THE AFGHAN BOOK

Design by Marion Graham

Maumelle, Arkansas • Leisure Arts Inc.

designs by Marion Graham

INTRODUCTION

This book contains a variety of afghans in several different techniques: knitting, crochet, broomstick lace, woven crochet, and afghan stitch. We have included complete instructions for beginners in the last three listed skills, and hope if you've not tried them before, you may wish to experiment with them.

Instructions for several different techniques — such as fringing, embroidering on afghan stitch, etc., apply to more than one afghan in the book. We have therefore grouped these in a section called **General Instructions** at the back of the book, and you may wish to read through these before beginning your work.

We know that you probably hate to make gauge swatches; and you may think that since an afghan doesn't have to fit anyone, if your gauge is a bit off, it won't matter. But it really will matter: if you're working too tightly, you'll get a smaller afghan than planned; and if too loosely, you may wind up with not enough yarn to complete the project. So please — take the few extra minutes needed to work up a 4" gauge swatch, in the pattern stitch specified, before you start any afghan. Change needle or hook size as needed to achieve the correct gauge.

If you have any difficulty understanding the instructions, or find any errors in any of the patterns, please write to us and we will make every effort to assist you. We would also enjoy hearing your comments on this book, and suggestions for other patterns you'd like to have us publish.

Janet Rondeau
Design Director

ABBREVIATIONS

Throughout the book, these abbreviations are used:

Knitting Abbreviations
CO — cast on
BO — bind off
K — knit
P — purl
tog — together
PSSO — pass slipped stitch over
Garter st — knit every row
Stock st — K1 row, P1 row

Crochet Abbreviations
ch — chain
sc — single crochet
dc — double crochet
hdc — half double crochet
tr — triple crochet
sl st — slip stitch

Abbreviations for Both Knitting and Crochet

st — stitch	inc — increase	rep — repeat (ing)
sts — stitches	dec — decrease	rem — remain (ing)
sp — space	beg — beginning	rnd — round
sk — skip	YO — yarn over	sl — slip
MC — Main Color		

( ) — Parentheses are used in two ways: first, to indicate steps to be worked the exact number of times specified immediately following the parentheses, as: (K2, P 6, K2) 3 times; and second, to clarify a group of sts to be worked all in the same space or stitch, as: (3 dc, ch 1, 3 dc) all in same sp.

TABLE OF CONTENTS

MOHAIR & WORSTED CABLE KNIT AFGHAN

Approx. size before fringing: 42" x 60"

MATERIALS

Worsted weight yarn:
- Solid color - 20 ounces
- Ombre color mohair - 11, 2-oz. skeins **OR**
- Entire afghan may be worked with double strand of worsted weight yarn using 10, 4-oz. skeins

29" Circular knitting needle, size 11 (Canadian size 1) **or** size needed for gauge

Cable needle

Gauge: 5 sts = 2" (in seed stitch)

PATTERN STITCH

SEED STITCH

Row 1: K1, ★ P1, K1; rep from ★ across as many sts as specified.
Rep Row 1 for pattern.

Note: Borders of afghan, and areas between cables, are worked in seed stitch.

INSTRUCTIONS

Using one strand of worsted and one of mohair (or 2 strands of worsted throughout, if preferred), CO 111 sts.

BORDER

Work even in seed st until piece measures 2½".

Increase Row (Wrong side)**:** Work in seed st across 9 sts, ★ P6, work in seed st across 5 sts; rep from ★ to last 14 sts, inc in next st, P4, work in seed st across 9 sts: 112 sts.

BODY PATTERN

Patt Row 1 (Right side)**:** Work in seed st across 9 sts, K6, ★ work in seed st across 5 sts, K6; rep from ★ to last 9 sts, work in seed st across 9 sts.

Patt Rows 2, 4, 6, 8, 10 and 12: Work in seed st across 9 sts, P6, ★ work in seed st across 5 sts, P6; rep from ★ to last 9 sts, work in seed st across 9 sts.

Patt Row 3: Work in seed st across 9 sts, K6, ★ work in seed st across 5 sts, K6; rep from ★ to last 9 sts, work in seed st across 9 sts.

Patt Row 5: Work in seed st across 9 sts, slip next 3 sts onto cable needle and hold in **back** of work, K3, K3 from cable needle, ★ work in seed st across 5 sts, slip next 3 sts onto cable needle and hold in **back** of work, K3, K3 from cable needle; rep from ★ to last 9 sts, work in seed st across 9 sts.

Patt Rows 7, 9 and 11: Work in seed st across 9 sts, K6, ★ work in seed st across 5 sts, K6; rep from ★ to last 9 sts, work in seed st across 9 sts.

Rep Patt Rows 1-12 until piece measures 58", ending by working Patt Row 9.

BORDER

Decrease Row (Wrong side)**:** Work in seed st across 9 sts, ★ P6, work in seed st across 5 sts; rep from ★ to last 15 sts, P2 tog, P4, work seed st across 9 sts: 111 sts.

Work even in seed st for 2½".

BO loosely.

FRINGE

Cut strands 10" long. Using 2 strands worsted and 2 strands mohair, (or 4 strands worsted), and following Basic Fringe Instructions on page 34, tie a tassel in every other st across short ends of afghan.

KNITTED CABLES & SQUARES AFGHAN

Approx. size before fringing: 42" x 65"

MATERIALS

Worsted Weight yarn:
Blue - 36 ounces
Knitting needles, size 9 (Canadian size 4)
or size needed for gauge
Cable needle
Stitch markers - 2

Gauge: In stock st, 4 sts = 1"; 11 rows = 2"

PATTERN STITCHES

CABLE PATTERN (worked over 14 sts)
Row 1: K2, P2, K6, P2, K2.

Row 2 and all even rows: K1, P1, K2, P6, K2, P1, K1.

Row 3: Rep Row 1.

Row 5 (Cable twist)**:** K2, P2, slip next 3 sts onto cable needle and hold in back of work; K3, K3 sts from cable needle, P2, K2.

Rows 7 and 9: K2, P2, K6, P2, K2.

Row 11 (Cable twist)**:** K2, P2, slip next 3 sts onto cable needle and hold in back of work; K3, K3 sts from cable needle, P2, K2.

Rows 13 and 15: K2, P2, K6, P2, K2.

Row 17 (Cable twist)**:** K2, P2, slip next 3 sts onto cable needle and hold in back of work; K3, K3 sts from cable needle, P2, K2.

Rows 19, 21, 23, 25, 27 and 29: K2, P2, K6, P2, K2.

Row 30: K1, P1, K2, P6, K2, P1, K1.

ALTERNATING SQUARES PATTERN (worked over 35 sts)
Row 1: ★ K7, P7, rep from ★ ending K7.

Row 2: ★ P7, K7, rep from ★ ending P7.

Rows 3-10: Rep Rows 1 and 2, 4 times.

Row 11 (reversing row)**:** ★ P7, K7, rep from ★ ending P7.

Row 12: ★ K7, P7, rep from ★ ending K7.

Rows 13-20: Rep Rows 11 and 12, 4 times.

Rep Rows 1-20 for pattern.

INSTRUCTIONS

PANELS (Make 3)
CO 63 sts. Work Row 1 of Cable Pattern over first 14 sts, place marker; work Row 1 of Alternating Squares Pattern over next 35 sts, place marker; work Row 1 of Cable Pattern over last 14 sts.

Continue to follow pattern rows, working Cable Pattern Rows 1—30 twelve times, then Rows 1—20 once; at same time continue Alternating Squares Pattern as established. BO loosely.

FINISHING

With **right** sides facing, sew strips together along the long sides. Lightly steam seams, if desired.

FRINGE

For fringe, cut strands of yarn 18" long.
Following Basic Fringe Instructions on page 34, using 5 strands in each tassel, knot tassels about every 4th st across each short end.

Tie double row of knots as shown in fringe instructions.

CLASSIC GRANNY SQUARE AFGHAN

Approx. size before fringing: 40" x 67"

MATERIALS

Worsted weight yarn:
- Black - 22 ounces
- Various scrap colors of your choice - 24 ounces **total**

Crochet hook, size H (Canadian size 5)
or size needed for gauge

Note: In our afghan, Black is the main color and a variety of yarn leftovers were also used. Each square is a different color combination, but each has Black for the 6th, 7th, 14th and 15th rnds.

Ombre yarns were used for the 10th and 11th rnds of 8 of the Squares. It will take a total of about 21 ounces. of various colored yarn, **plus** the black, to complete the afghan.

Gauge: 15-rnd square = 12½"

INSTRUCTIONS

GRANNY SQUARE (Make 15)
Following Basic Granny Square Instructions on page 35, make 15-rnd Granny Squares in these colors:

Rnds 1-5: Colors of your choice.

Rnds 6 and 7: Black.

Rnds 8-13: Colors of your choice.

Rnds 14 and 15: Black.

ASSEMBLING
Join Squares in a rectangle, 3 squares by 5 squares, using your choice of joining method ***(see page 34)***.

FINISHING
Join Black in any corner space and work 2 rnds around entire afghan, following Rnd 4 of Basic Granny Square Instructions.

BROWN-EYED SUSAN IN AFGHAN STITCH

Approx. size before fringing: 45" x 60"

MATERIALS

Worsted Weight yarn:

White - 40 ounces
Bright Yellow - 12 ounces
Med. Olive Green - 8 ounces
Rust - 4 ounces

Afghan Hook, size J (Canadian size 3) **or** size needed for gauge

Crochet hook, size H (Canadian size 5)

Gauge: In afghan st, 4 sts = 1; 3 rows = 1"

AFGHAN STITCH BLOCKS (Make 35)

With afghan hook and White, ch 25. Following Basic Afghan St instructions on page 36, work 18 rows afghan st (remember that foundation row counts as a row), ending on right-hand side of block with second half of last row; one loop remains on hook.

Slip this loop onto crochet hook, skip first bar, slip st in each bar across row to last bar; in last bar, for corner work (sc, ch 2, sc).

EDGING

Rnd 1: ★ Work 17 sc across next side of block, work (sc, ch 2, sc) in corner; rep from ★ twice; work 17 sc across last side (top of block), sc in corner ch-2 sp.

(Note: when working across bottom and top sides of block, you will have to skip a few sts, evenly spaced, to have 17 sc).

Rnd 2: Ch 2, sc in corner ch-2 sp, ★ sc in each sc to corner, (sc, ch 2, sc) in corner. Rep from ★ to last side, sc in each sc across to corner, join with a sl st in 2nd ch of beg ch. You should have 19 sc along each side, not counting (sc, ch 2, sc) in corners.
Finish off, turn.

Rnd 3: Join Yellow with slip st in any corner ch-2 sp, rep Rnd 2. Do **not** finish off, turn.

Rnd 4: Rep Rnd 2. Finish off, turn.

Rnd 5: Join Olive with sl st into any corner ch-2 sp, rep Rnd 2, finish off. You should have 25 sc along each side, not counting (sc, ch 2, sc) in corners. Mark top of each Block. Always keep marked side of block at top while embroidering.

EMBROIDERY

Following Cross Stitch instructions on page 35, embroider 18 blocks with large brown-eyed Susans ***(Chart A)***. Find center stitch of Block and start embroidering with Rust at center st, marked on Chart A. Then, work a small motif ***(Chart B)*** in all 4 corners of rem 17 Blocks, placing each motif 2 rows down from top or up from bottom and 2 bars in from left or right.

ASSEMBLING

Join White in any ch-2 corner sp of any block.

Rnd A: Sc, ch 2, sc in same sp, ★ sc in each sc to corner, (sc, ch 2, sc) in corner. Rep from ★ 2 times, sc across last side, join with a slip st to first sc. You should have 27 sc along each side, not counting (sc, ch 2, sc) in corners. Do **not** turn.

Rnd B: Slip st in ch-2 sp, (sc, ch 3, sc) in same sp, ch 3, ★ sk 1 sc, sc in next sc, sk 1 sc, ch 3. Rep from ★ around, working (sc, ch 3, sc) in each ch-2 corner sp. Join with a slip st to first sc. Finish off.

Work Rnds A and B around every Block.

Arrange Blocks on floor in position shown in ***Fig. 1***. Make sure top of each Block faces same direction, up. Place Blocks 1 and 2 with right sides tog ***(Fig. 2)***.

FIG. 1

A29	B22	A15	B8	A1
B30	A23	B16	A9	B2
A31	B24	A17	B10	A3
B32	A25	B18	A11	B4
A33	B26	A19	B12	A5
B34	A27	B20	A13	B6
A35	B28	A21	B14	A7

FIG. 2

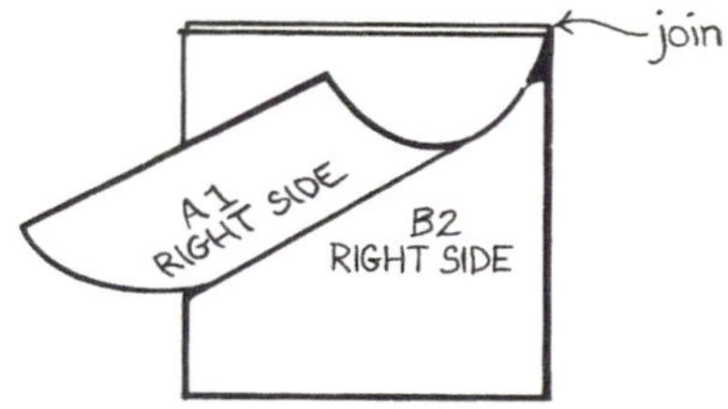

Joining Rnd: Join White with slip st in upper right-hand corner sp of front Block, ch 1, sc in corner sp of back Block, ★ ch 1, sc in next ch-3 sp of front Block, ch 1, sc in next ch-3 sp of back Block; rep from ★ across side, ch 1, sc in corner sp of front Block, ch 1, sc in corner sp of back Block. Finish off.

Following placement shown in ***Fig. 1***, join Blocks 3, 4, 5, 6 & 7 in same manner. Join rem Blocks into 4 more strips, then join strips in same way, being sure to work into all 4 corners at intersections of Blocks.

FRINGE

Follow Basic Fringe Instructions on page 34. Each tassel contains five 10" strands of White. Place one in every ch-3 sp on the ends.

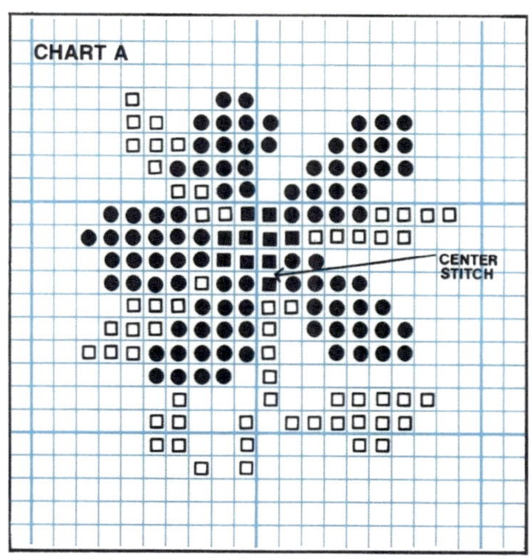

CHART B

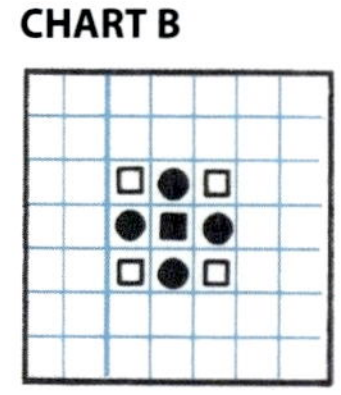

bright yellow ● **rust** ■
med olive □

TURQUOISE MOHAIR & WOOL BOBBLE CROCHET AFGHAN

Approx. size before fringing: 46" x 64"

MATERIALS

Worsted Weight yarn:
Turquoise - 22 ounces
Turquoise mohair - 24 ounces
or entire afghan may be worked with 44 ounces worsted
Crochet hook, size K (Canadian size 2)
or size needed for gauge

Gauge: 2 dc = 1"; 5 dc rows = 4"

Special Note: Outer row of Bobbles is worked in Finishing. Always count turning ch 3 as one dc, and work with 1 strand of mohair and 1 strand of worsted, **or** 2 strands of worsted held tog, throughout.

INSTRUCTIONS

Ch 93 very loosely.

Row 1: Dc in 4th ch from hook and in each ch to end: you should have 91 dcs.

Row 2: Ch 3, turn; dc in each dc across.

Row 3: Ch 3, turn; dc in each of next 4 dc, ★ 5 dc in next dc, drop loop from hook, insert hook through top of first st of the 5-dc group, hook dropped loop and draw through ***(Fig. 1)***, ch 1 **(one Bobble made)**; dc in each of next 3 dc. Rep from ★ to within 6 dc of end. Work a bobble in next dc, dc in each of last 5 dc: you should have 21 bobbles.

FIG. 1

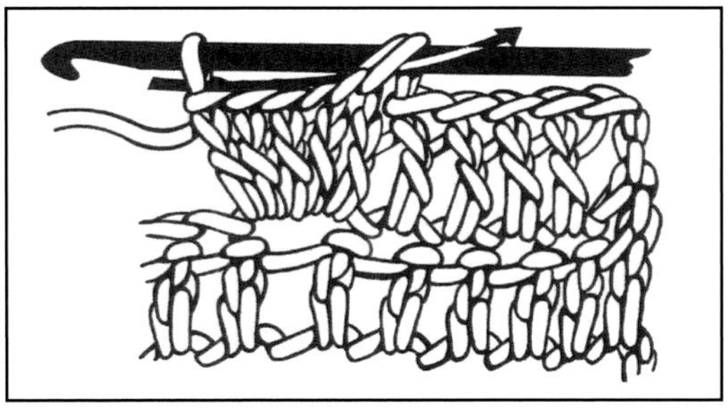

Row 4: Ch 3, turn; dc in each of next 4 dc, dc in top of Bobble. ★ Ch 1, sk one dc, dc in next dc, ch 1, sk one dc, dc in top of Bobble; rep from ★ to within 5 sts of end, dc in each of last 5 dc.

Row 5: Ch 3, turn; dc in each of next 4 dc, Bobble in next dc. ★ Ch 1, dc in next dc; rep from ★ to within 6 sts of end, ch 1, Bobble in next dc, dc in each of last 5 dc.

Row 6: Ch 3, turn; dc in each of next 4 dc, dc in Bobble. ★ Ch 1, dc in next dc; rep from ★ to within 6 sts of end, ch 1, dc in Bobble, dc in each of last 5 dc.

Rows 7-18: Rep Rows 5 and 6, 6 times **more**.

Row 19: Ch 3, turn; dc in each of next 4 dc, Bobble in next dc, (ch 1, dc in next dc) 11 times, ch 1. ★ Bobble in next dc, dc in next ch-1 sp, dc in next dc, dc in next ch-1 sp; rep from ★ 7 times. Bobble in next dc, (ch 1, dc in next dc) 11 times, ch 1, Bobble in next dc, dc in each of last 5 dc.

Row 20: Ch 3, turn; dc in each of next 4 dc, dc in Bobble, (ch 1, dc in next dc) 11 times, ch 1. ★ Dc in bobble, dc in each of next 3 dc; rep from ★ 7 times. Dc in Bobble, (ch 1, dc in next dc) 11 times, ch 1, dc in Bobble, dc in each of last 5 dc.

Row 21: Ch 3, turn; dc in each of next 4 dc, Bobble in next dc, (ch 1, dc in next dc) 11 times, ch 1. Bobble in next dc, dc in each of next 31 dc. Bobble in next dc, (ch 1, dc in next dc) 11 times, ch 1, Bobble in next dc, dc in each of last 5 dc.

Row 22: Ch 3, turn; dc in each of next 4 dc, dc in Bobble, (ch 1, dc in next dc) 11 times, ch 1. Dc in Bobble, dc in each of next 31 dc. Dc in Bobble, (ch 1, dc in next dc) 11 times, ch 1, dc in Bobble, dc in each of last 5 dc.

Row 23: Ch 3, turn; dc in each of next 4 dc, Bobble in next dc, (ch 1, dc in next dc) 11 times, ch 1. Bobble in next dc, dc in each of next 7 dc. ★ Bobble in next dc, dc in each of next 3 dc; rep from ★ 3 times **more**. Bobble in next dc, dc in each of next 7 dc. Bobble in next dc, (ch 1, dc in next dc) 11 times, ch 1, Bobble in next dc, dc in each of last 5 dc.

Row 24: Ch 3, turn; dc in each of next 4 dc, dc in Bobble, (ch 1, dc in next dc) 11 times, ch 1. Dc in Bobble, dc in each of next 7 dc, dc in Bobble. ★ Ch 1, sk one dc, dc in next dc, ch 1, sk one dc, dc in Bobble; rep from ★ 3 times **more**. Dc in each of next 7 dc, dc in Bobble, (ch 1, dc in next dc) 11 times, ch 1, dc in Bobble, dc in each of last 5 dc.

Row 25: Ch 3, turn ; dc in each of next 4 dc, Bobble in next dc, (ch 1, dc in next dc) 11 times, ch 1. Bobble in next dc, dc in each of next 7 dc, Bobble in next dc. ★ Ch 1, dc in next dc; rep from ★ 6 times, ch 1. Bobble in next dc, dc in each of next 7 dc. Bobble in next dc, (ch 1, dc in next dc) 11 times, ch 1, Bobble in next dc, dc in each of last 5 dc.

Row 26: Ch 3, turn; dc in each of next 4 dc, dc in Bobble, (ch 1, dc in next dc) 11 times. Ch 1, dc in Bobble, dc in each of next 7 dc, dc in Bobble. ★ Ch 1, dc in next dc; rep from ★ 6 times. Ch 1, dc in Bobble, dc in each of next 7 dc, dc in Bobble, (ch 1, dc in next dc) 11 times, ch 1, dc in Bobble, dc in each of last 5 dc.

Rows 27-56: Rep Rows 25 and 26, 15 times **more**.

Row 57: Ch 3, turn; dc in each of next 4 dc, Bobble in next dc, (ch 1, dc in next dc) 11 times. Ch 1, Bobble in next dc, dc in each of next 7 dc. ★ Bobble in next dc, dc in ch-1 sp, dc in next dc, dc in ch-1 sp; rep from ★ 3 times. Bobble in next dc, dc in each of next 7 dc, Bobble in next dc, (ch 1, dc in next dc) 11 times, ch 1, Bobble in next dc, dc in each of last 5 dc.

Row 58: Ch 3, turn; dc in each of next 4 dc, dc in Bobble, (ch 1, dc in next dc) 11 times. Ch 1, dc in Bobble, dc in each of next 7 dc. * Dc in Bobble, dc in each of next 3 dc; rep from ★ 3 times. Dc in Bobble, dc in each of next 7 dc, dc in Bobble, (ch 1, dc in next dc) 11 times, ch 1, dc in Bobble, dc in each of last 5 dc.

Rows 59 and 60: Rep Rows 21 and 22.

Row 61: Ch 3, turn; dc in each of next 4 dc, Bobble in next dc, (ch 1, dc in next dc) 11 times, ch 1. ★ Bobble in next dc, dc in each of next 3 dc; rep from ★ 7 times. Bobble in next dc, (ch 1, dc in next dc) 11 times, ch 1, Bobble in next dc, dc in each of last 5 dc.

Row 62: Ch 3, turn; dc in each of next 4 dc, dc in Bobble, (ch 1, dc in next dc) 11 times, ch 1. ★ Dc in Bobble, ch 1, sk one dc, dc in next dc, ch 1; rep from ★ 7 times. Dc in Bobble, (ch 1, dc in next dc) 11 times, ch 1, dc in Bobble, dc in each of last 5 dc.

Rows 63-76: Rep Rows 5 and 6, 7 times.

Row 77: Ch 3, turn; dc in each of next 4 dc. ★ Bobble in next dc, dc in ch-1 sp, dc in next dc, dc in ch-1 sp; rep from ★ to within 6 sts of end, Bobble in next dc, dc in each of last 5 dc.

Row 78: Ch 3, turn; dc in each of next 4 dc. ★ Dc in Bobble, dc in each of next 3 dc; rep from ★ to within 6 sts of end, dc in Bobble, dc in each of last 5 sts.

Row 79: Rep Row 2. Finish off.

FINISHING

Border Row: With **right** side facing and short end at top, join 2 strands yarn in first dc at upper right-hand corner, ch 3, 4 dc in same space; Bobble in next dc. ★ Dc in each of next 3 dc, Bobble in next dc; rep from ★ to last dc, 5 dc in last dc. Continue by working into rows down long side: Bobble in first row, ★★ 3 dc in next row, Bobble in next row; rep from ★★ across to last row, Bobble in last row. In first dc of 2nd short end work 5 dc, Bobble in next dc; rep from ★ to ★ ending by working 5 dc in last dc. In first row of 2nd long side, work Bobble; rep from ★★ to ★★ ending by joining with a slip st in top of beg ch-3. Finish off.

FRINGE

Follow Basic Fringe Instructions on page 34. Each tassel contains three 10" strands worsted and three 10" strands mohair or 6 strands worsted if mohair is not used. There are 48 tassels on each short end: one tied in every other dc.

COIN CABLE KNIT AFGHAN

Approx. size before fringing: 44" x 62"

MATERIALS

Worsted Weight yarn:
- Bright Yellow & Bright Orange - 16 ounces **each** color
- Rust - 14 ounces

Knitting needles, size 7 (Canadian size 6) **or** size needed for gauge
Cable needle
Tapestry needle

Gauge: Each wide strip = 4½" wide;
Each narrow strip = 1½" wide

Note: For ease in counting garter stitch rows, 2 rows = 1 ridge.

INSTRUCTIONS

WIDE PANELS (Make 4 Yellow & 3 Rust)
CO 24 sts and knit 10 rows (5 garter st ridges).

Pattern Row 1: K6, P2, K8, P2, K6.

Row 2 and all even rows: K5, P1, K2, P8, K2, P1, K5.

Row 3: K6, P2, slip next 2 sts to cable needle and hold in **back** of work, K2, K2 from cable needle; slip next 2 sts to cable needle and hold in **front** of work, K2, K2 from cable needle, P2, K6.

Rows 5, 7 and 9: K6, P2, K8, P2, K6.

Row 11: K6, P2, sl next 2 sts to cable needle and hold in **front** of work, K2, K2 from cable needle; sl next 2 sts to cable needle, hold in **back** of work, K2, K2 from cable needle; P2, K6.

Rows 13 and 15: K6, P2, K8, P2, K6.

Row 16: K5, P1, K2, P8, K2, P1, K5.

Rep Rows 1-16, 25 times, then rep Rows 1-14 once.

Knit 10 rows (5 garter st ridges).

BO loosely.

NARROW PANELS (Make 8 Orange)
CO 7 sts.

Knit 450 rows (225 garter st ridges).

BO loosely.

ASSEMBLING

Sew an Orange Panel to **each** side of every Yellow Panel, carefully matching rows.

Place all Panels out on floor side by side lengthwise.

Starting at left side, arrange in this order:

Yellow/Orange, Rust; Yellow/Orange, Rust;
Yellow/Orange, Rust; Yellow/Orange.

Sew Panels together, carefully matching rows.

FRINGE

Following Basic Fringe Instructions on page 34, cut Orange strands 10" long.

Tie tassels of 5 strands each every third st across each end.

GOLD AND WHITE MEDALLION AFGHAN

Approx. size before fringing: 40" x 58"

MATERIALS

Worsted Weight yarn:
Gold - 20 ounces
White - 16 ounces
Crochet hook, size I (Canadian size 4)
or size needed for gauge

Gauge: Each medallion = 8½" square

INSTRUCTIONS

MEDALLIONS (Make 24)
With Gold, ch 6, join with a slip st to form a ring.

Rnd 1: Ch 2, 11 sc into ring, join with a slip st to 2nd ch of beg ch 2.

Rnd 2: Ch 4, (dc, ch 1) in each sc around: you should have 12 ch-1 sps. Join with a slip st to 3rd ch of beg ch-4.

Rnd 3 (Puff St Rnd)**:** Draw up loop on hook to ¾", (YO, insert hook in first dc, draw up a ¾" loop) 5 times: 11 loops on hook; YO, draw through all 11 loops, ch 3 **(1 Puff St made)**. Work 1 Puff St in each dc around: 12 Puff Sts. Join with a slip st in top of first Puff St.

Rnd 4: Ch 2,★ work 2 sc in ch-3 sp, sc in top of Puff St, rep from ★ around ending 2 sc in ch-3 sp, join with a slip st to beg ch-2: you should have 36 sc.

Rnd 5: Ch 4 **(counts as a dc plus ch 1)**, (dc, ch 1) in each sc around: 36 dc. Join with a slip st in third ch of beg ch-4.

Rnd 6: Ch 2, sc in each dc and each ch-1 sp around: 72 sc. Join with a sl st to beg ch 2. Finish off Gold. Join white in any sc.

Rnd 7: Ch 6, tr in same sc **(corner made)**. ★ Tr in next sc, dc in next 3 sc, hdc in next 3 sc, sc in next 3 sc, hdc in next 3 sc, dc in next 3 sc, tr in next sc, (tr, ch 2, tr) in next sc **(corner made)**. Rep from ★ 2 times **more**; tr in next sc, dc in next 3 sc, hdc in next 3 sc, sc in next 3 sc, hdc in next 3 sc, dc in next 3 sc, tr in next sc, join with a slip st to 4th ch of beg ch-6.

Rnd 8: Ch 3, turn. Dc in next 3 sts, (hdc in next 3 sts, sc in next 5 sts, hdc in next 3 sts, dc in next 4 sts, [dc, ch 2, dc] in corner ch-2 sp, dc in each of the next 4 sts) 3 times; ending hdc in next 3 sts, sc in next 5 sts, hdc in next 3 sts, dc in next 4 sts, work (dc, ch 2, dc) in last corner sp; join with a slip st to 3rd ch of beg ch-3.

Rnd 9: Ch 3, turn, dc in next st, ([dc, ch 2, dc} in corner ch-2 sp, dc in next 21 sts) 3 times; (dc, ch 2, dc) in next corner sp, 1 dc in each of last 19 sts, join with a slip st to 3rd ch of beg ch 3.

Finish off.

EDGING
Join Gold in any ch-2 corner space of any Medallion.

Rnd 1: Ch 5, dc in same sp, ★ (ch 1, skip 1 dc, dc in next dc) 11 times, ch 1, work (dc, ch 2, dc) in corner ch-2 sp. Rep from ★ 2 times **more**, ending (ch 1, skip 1 dc, dc in next dc) 11 times, ch 1, join with a slip st to 3rd ch of beg ch-5.

Rnd 2: Slip st into ch-2 corner sp, ch 4, sc in same sp, (★ ch 3, sc in next ch-1 sp, rep from ★ to corner, ch 3, work 1 sc, ch 3, 1 sc in ch-2 corner sp) 3 times. ★★ Ch 3, sc in next ch-1 sp, rep from ★★ to corner, ch 3, join with a slip st to 2nd ch of beg ch 4. Finish off.

Work Rnds 1 and 2 around all Medallions.

JOINING MEDALLIONS
Place 2 Medallions with **right** sides together. Join Gold with sc in upper right-hand corner sp of front Medallion, ch 1, sc in corner sp of back Medallion; ★ ch 1, sc in next ch-3 sp of front Medallion, ch 1, sc in next ch-3 sp of back Medallion, rep from ★ across side; ch 1, sc in corner sp of front Medallion, ch 1, sc in corner sp of back Medallion. Finish off.

Using same joining method, make 4 strips of 6 Medallions each. Join strips in same way along long sides, being sure to work into all 4 corners at intersections of Medallions.
Finished afghan is 4 Medallions wide and 6 Medallions long.

FRINGE
Follow Basic Fringe Instructions on page 34, alternating Gold and White tassels. Each Gold tassel contains five 10" strands Gold; each White tassel contains four 10" strands White.
There are 55 tassels on each end: one in each ch-3 space.

OFF-WHITE GRANNY SQUARE AFGHAN

Approx. size before fringing: 45" x 64"

MATERIALS

Worsted Weight yarn:
- Off-White - 24 ounces
- Brown, Rust, Lt. Olive, Coral, Yellow & Med. Blue - 6 oz. **each** color

Crochet hook, size I (Canadian size 4) **or** size needed for gauge

Gauge: 9-rnd square = 9"

INSTRUCTIONS

Following Basic Granny Square Instructions on page 35, make a total of 23, 9-rnd squares in the following combinations:

COMBINATION:	**A (Make 11)**	**B (Make 12)**
Rnd 1	Off-White	Off-White
Rnd 2	Brown	Med. Blue
Rnd 3	Rust	Yellow
Rnd 4	Lt. Olive	Coral
Rnd 5	Coral	Lt. Olive
Rnd 6	Yellow	Rust
Rnd 7	Med. Blue	Brown
Rnds 8 & 9	Off-White	Off-White

ASSEMBLING

CENTER PANEL

Using your choice of joining methods on page 34, join one Block A to one Block B.
Join second Block B to opposite side of Block A.
This forms center panel.

EDGING

With **right** side of work facing, join Off-White in any ch-1 corner sp of center panel. Ch 3, (2 dc, ch 1, 3 dc) in same sp, ch 1, (3 dc, ch 1) in each ch-1 sp across, working (3 dc, ch 1) in each corner of each square, but not in the joining space between squares, and (3 dc, ch 1, 3 dc) in each of 3 rem corners of center panel. You should have 10 3-dc groups on each short end and 30 3-dc groups on **each** side, counting one group at each corner.

Work one **more** rnd in Off-White, then 1 rnd **each** in the following color sequence: Med Blue, Yellow, Coral, Lt Olive, Rust and Brown.

Work 2 rnds **more** in Off-White. Then work 1 rnd **each**, reversing color sequence above.

Work 2 rnds **more** in Off-White; finish off.

JOINING OUTER PANELS

Using same joining method, join 3 squares to form one end panel, with a Block B in the center and one Block A on either side of it.

Join 3 more squares in same manner to form other end panel. You should have 27 3-dc groups along each short end of center panel and along edge of each end panel to be joined.

Join one end panel at each short end of center panel, carefully matching sts. Now join 7 squares, beg with a Block B and alternating with Block A to form a side panel ***(Fig. 1)***. Join rem 7 squares in same manner for other side panel. You should have 63 3-dc groups along joining edge of each side panel and there are now 65 3-dc groups along center panel edge to be joined.

FIG. 1

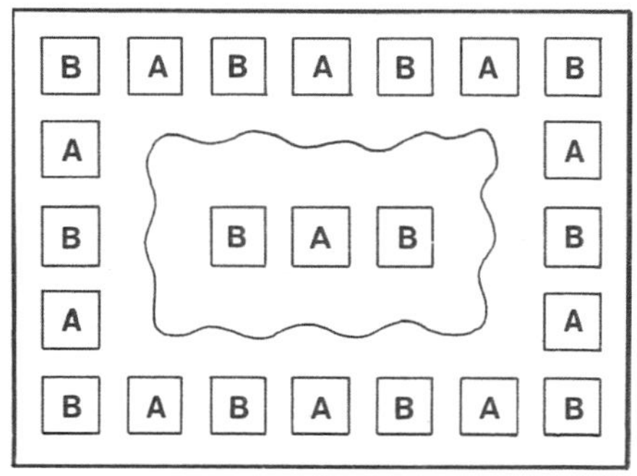

To join side panel, beg by joining first 2 squares of side panel to center panel carefully matching sts, then join next 3-dc group of center panel in joining seam between 2nd and 3rd square of side panel. Continue matching sts and joining next 3 squares of side panel, then join next 3-dc group of center panel in joining seam between 5th and 6th square of side panel, join rem 2 squares matching sts.

Join other side panel in same manner. Then, join Off-White with a slip st and work 2 rnds, following Basic Granny Square Instructions for Rnd 4, around entire afghan. Finish off.

FRINGE

Follow Basic Fringe Instructions on page 34. Each tassel contains five 12" long strands. You will need 48 tassels for each end; place one in each corner sp and one between each 3-dc group.

BLACK & WHITE GRANNY ZEBRA STRIPE AFGHAN

Approx. size before fringing: 46" x 65"

MATERIALS

Worsted Weight yarn:
- Black - 28 ounces
- White - 14 ounces

Crochet hook, size I (Canadian size 4) **or** size needed for gauge.

Gauge: 6-rnd granny square = 6"
3 rows dc = 2"; 3 dc = 1"

Notes: You will first make seven 6-rnd granny squares, joining them as they are being completed, to form one long strip which runs the length of the afghan in the center ***(see Fig. 1)***.

FIG. 1

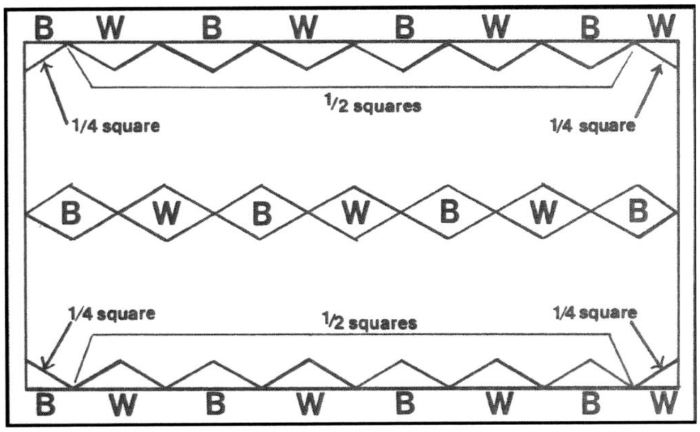

Use the Basic Granny Square instructions on page 35 for Rnds 1-3. After Rnd 3, work ch 1 in corner spaces only; do **not** work ch 1 between 3-dc groups on sides of square.

In ***Fig. 1***, squares are identified as **B** or **W.**

A black center square (**B)** is worked as follows:
Rnd 1: Black; **Rnds 2 and 3:** White; **Rnds 4-6:** Black.
A white center square **(W)** is worked as follows:
Rnds 1-3: White; **Rnds 4-6:** Black.

Make 4 black center squares and 3 white center squares.

INSTRUCTIONS

Work one complete **B** square. Next work one **W** square up to the 4th corner of last rnd. In 4th corner sp, work 3 dc, pick up **B** square and join it by working a slip st into any corner ch-1 sp (be sure to keep right side of work facing); drop **B** square, 3 dc in same corner ch-1 sp of **W** square to complete corner; finish **W** square in usual manner. Set these joined squares aside, and work another **B** square up to 4th corner sp of last rnd. In 4th corner sp, work 3 dc, pick up joined squares, slip st into the 2nd corner ch-1 sp of joined **W** square (opposite prev joining), 3 dc in same corner ch-1 sp of **B** square; finish **B** square in usual manner. Continue in this way, alternating **W** and **B** squares, until you have 7 in a row (check placement indicated in ***Fig. 1)***.

RIPPLE STRIPES

With **right** side of joined squares facing, and strip of squares held horizontally, join white in corner ch-1 sp at right of first square.

Row 1: Ch 3, from now on working in **back loop only** (loop away from you), (YO, insert hook in **next** dc, pull up a loop, YO and pull through 2 loops on hook) twice, YO and pull through all 3 loops on hook **(dec made)**; ★ dc in each of next 16 dc, 5 dc in ch-1 sp (inc made); dc in each of next 16 dc, dec over next 5 sts as follows ***(Note:*** in this row **only**, the third st of the next 5 sts is the slip st worked to join squares.): (YO, insert hook in **next** st, pull up a loop, YO and pull through 2 loops on hook) 5 times: 6 loops on hook. YO and pull through all 6 loops **(dec made)**. Rep from ★ to within 2 sts of end, dec over last 2 dc, dc in corner ch-1 sp; ch 3, turn.

Row 2: Dec over next 3 sts as follows: (YO, insert hook in **next** dc, pull up a loop, YO and pull through 2 loops on hook) 3 times: 4 loops on hook. YO and pull through all 4 loops **(dec made)**; ★ dc in each of next 16 dc, 5 dc in 3rd dc of inc of prev row, dc in each of next 16 dc, dec over next 5 sts, rep from ★ across to within 4 sts of end, dec over next 3 sts, dc in ch 3; ch 3, turn.

Rep Row 2 eighteen times, working (4 rows black, 2 rows white) 3 times. Finish off.

Join white in same manner on opposite side of squares, work same as first side. Finish off.

Following instructions below, make 12 half squares:
6 with white centers (**W)** and 6 with black centers **(B**).

GRANNY HALF SQUARES

Row 1: Ch 4, (3 dc, ch 1, 4 dc) in first ch, turn.

Row 2: Ch 3 **(counts as first dc)**, 3 dc in next dc, (3 dc, ch 1, 3 dc) in ch-1 sp, 4 dc in top of turning ch, turn.

Row 3: Ch 3, 3 dc in next dc, 3 dc in next side sp, (3 dc, ch 1, 3 dc) in ch-1 sp, 3 dc in next side sp, 4 dc in top of turning ch, turn.

Rows 4-6: Rep Row 3, adding one 3-dc group each side every row.

Following instructions below, make 4 quarter squares:
2 with white centers (**W**) and 2 with black centers (**B**).

GRANNY QUARTER SQUARES

Row 1: Ch 4, 4 dc in first ch, turn.

Row 2: Ch 3, 3 dc in first dc, 4 dc in top of turning ch, turn.

Row 3: Ch 3, 3 dc in first dc, 3 dc in next side sp, 4 dc in top of turning ch, turn.

Rows 4-6: Rep Row 3, adding one 3-dc group each row.

FINISHING

Following placement shown in ***Fig. 1***, sew half and quarter squares to outer edges of ripples at side edges, carefully matching sts.

Border: With **right** side of work facing, join black at right-hand corner on a long side of afghan.

Row 1: Ch 3, and carefully spacing sts to keep work flat, work in dc along entire side, working in sides of granny squares, and placing a dc in center st of each ripple point; ch 3, turn.

Rows 2-4: Working in **back loop only**, dc in each dc across.

Finish off. Work opposite side the same.

Fringe: Following Basic Fringe Instructions on page 34, cut 12" strands of black and white. Using 5 strands in each tassel, knot a tassel in each row at each end, white tassel in each white row, black tassel in each black row.

GREEN BOBBLE KNIT CHILD'S AFGHAN

Approx. size: 38" x 46"

MATERIALS

Worsted Weight yarn:
Green - 20 ounces
Knitting needles, size 9 (Canadian size 4)
or size needed for gauge

Gauge: In pattern, 4 sts = 1"

Note: In this pattern the abbreviation "SSK" means to work as follows: Slip the first and second sts knitwise, one at a time, then insert the tip of left-hand needle into the front of these 2 sts from the **left**, and knit them together from this position.

BOBBLE PATTERN

Row 1 (Right side): P1, ★ YO, SSK, P5, K2 tog, YO, P1; rep from ★.

Row 2: K1, ★ K1, P1, K5, P1, K2; rep from ★.

Row 3: P1, ★ P1, YO, SSK, P3, K2 tog, YO, P2; rep from ★.

Row 4: K1, ★ K2, P1, K3, P1, K3; rep from ★.

Row 5: P1, ★ P2, YO, SSK, P1, K2 tog, YO, P3; rep from ★.

Row 6: K1, ★ K3, P1, K1, P1, K4; rep from ★.

Row 7: P1, ★ P3, YO slip 2 knitwise, K1, pass the 2 slip sts over the knit st, YO, P3; make bobble in next st as follows: (K1, YO, K1, YO, K1) **all** in same st; **turn** and P5, **turn** and K5, **turn** and P5; **turn** and SSK, K1, K2 tog; **turn** and P3 tog, **turn** and with yarn in back slip bobble st to right-hand needle; rep from ★ across to last 10 sts, then P3, YO, slip 2 knitwise, K1, pass the 2 slip sts over the knit st, YO, P4.

Row 8: K1, ★ K3, P3, K3, P1 into **back** of bobble st; rep from ★ across to last 10 sts, then K3, P3, K4.

Row 9: P1, ★ P2, K2 tog, YO, P1, YO, SSK, P3; rep from ★.

Row 10: K1, ★ K2, P1, K3, P1, K3; rep from ★.

Row 11: P1, ★ P1, K2 tog, YO, P3, YO, SSK, P2; rep from ★.

Row 12: K1, ★ K1, P1, K5, P1, K2; rep from ★.

Row 13: P1, ★ K2 tog, YO, P5, YO, SSK, P1; rep from ★.

Row 14: K1, ★ P1, K7, P1, K1; rep from ★.

Row 15: K2 tog, ★ YO, P3, make bobble in next st (as in Row 7), P3, YO, slip 2 knitwise, K1, pass the 2 slip sts over the knit st; rep from ★ across to last 9 sts, then YO, P3, make bobble, P3, YO, SSK.

Row 16: P1, ★ P1, K3, P1 into **back** of bobble st, K3, P2; rep from ★.

Rep Rows 1-16 for pattern.

INSTRUCTIONS

CO 151 sts.

Row 1: K1, ★ P1, K1, rep from ★.

Rep Row 1 (Seed St) for 1½".

Keep 5 sts on each end in Seed St, and work Pattern Rows 1-16 on center 141 sts until piece measures 44½" from CO edge **or** desired length.

Work Seed St across entire afghan for 1½" border.

BO loosely.

BLUE PANELS EMBROIDERED AFGHAN

Approx. size before fringing: 51" x 62"

MATERIALS

Worsted weight yarn:
- Off-White - 20 ounces
- Navy Blue, Royal Blue, Dk. Blue, Med. Blue & Lt. Olive Green - 8 ounces **each** color
- Baby Blue - 4 ounces

14 " Afghan hook, size J (Canadian size 3) **or** size needed for gauge

Crochet hook, size H (Canadian size 5)

Gauge: In afghan stitch, 4 sts = 1"; 3 rows = 1"

INSTRUCTIONS

You will first make 7 strips in afghan stitch, one in baby blue and two each in royal blue, dk. and med. blue.

For each strip, following Basic Afghan Stitch Instructions on page 35, ch 17.

Pick up 17 loops, and work 189 afghan st rows; work binding off row, in sc instead of slip st; do **not** break yarn.

Slip loop on hook to crochet hook; in corner work (sc, ch 1, sc); sc in each row down long side, in corner work (sc, ch 1, sc); sc in each st along short end, work corner as before; sc in each row along second long side, work corner as before; join with slip st to binding off row. Finish off.

BORDERS

With **right** side of strip facing, join Lt. Olive at top corner ch-1 sp of either long side, sc in same sp, sc in each sc to bottom corner sp: 191 sc. Finish off.

Rep along opposite side.

Bobble Row: With **right** side of strip facing, join Off-White in first Lt. Olive sc at top corner. Ch 3, 4 dc in same sp; drop loop from hook, insert hook through 3rd ch of ch-3; pick up dropped loop and draw through tightly; ★ ch 2, skip 1 sc, 5 dc in next sc, drop loop from hook, insert hook through top of first st of 5-dc group, pick up dropped loop and draw through tightly **(bobble made)**; rep from ★ 94 times ending with a bobble in last sc space. Finish off.

Work Bobble Row in same manner along other side of strip. Attach Lt. Olive at top of first bobble of either side of strip, sc in same sp; ★ sc in ch-2 sp, sc in top of next bobble, rep from ★ ending sc in top of last bobble (191 sc). Fasten off Lt. Olive.

Repeat on opposite side of strip. Join Navy in firstLt. Olive sc at corner of either side of strip, sc in each sc to end. Fasten off.

Repeat on opposite side of strip.

EMBROIDERY

First see Cross Stitch Embroidery section on page 35. Then following chart in ***Fig. 1***, embroider strips, starting at bottom, as follows: on 2 Royal and 2 Med. Blue strips, work chart from Row A through Row B, rep from A through B up strip, ending last rep with Row C. On 2 Dk. Blue and the Baby Blue strip, work chart from Row D through Row B, then rep from A through B up strip, ending last rep with Row E.

FIG. 1

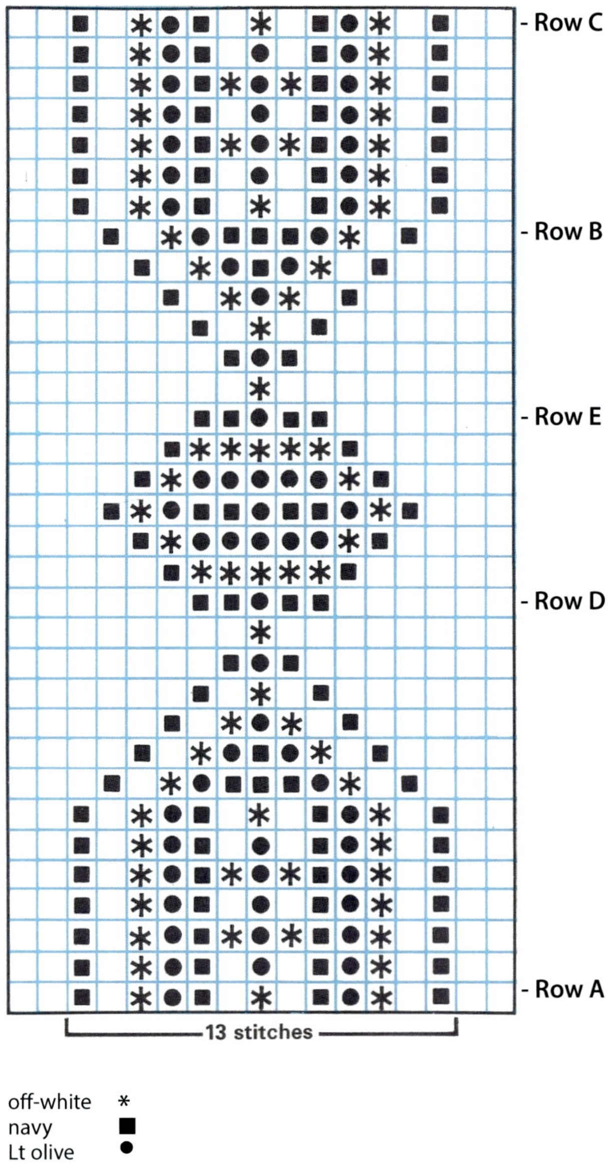

WOVEN PLAID CROCHET AFGHAN

Approx. size before fringing: 42" x 53"

MATERIALS

Worsted Weight yarn:
Black - 16 ounces
Kelly gGreen & Red - 8 ounces **each** color
White, Lt. Yellow & Royal Blue - 4 ounces **each** color
Crochet hook, size I (Canadian size 4)
or size needed for gauge
Large-eyed tapestry needle

Gauge: 5 dc and 4 sps = 2"
2 rows = 1"

Note: We suggest you weave in yarn ends as each mesh row is finished to avoid having to do them all at one time at the end.

INSTRUCTIONS

MESH BACKGROUND

With black, ch 188 very loosely.

Row 1: Dc in 4th ch from hook, ★ ch 1, skip 1 ch, dc in next ch. Rep from ★ across: 93 sps.

Row 2: Ch 4, turn. ★ Dc in top of next dc, ch 1. Rep from ★ across, ending dc in 3rd ch of turning ch.

Rep Row 2 for mesh background, changing colors as specified for Background Mesh Rows in ***Fig. 1.***

Rows 3-35: Follow colors in Mesh Chart Rows 3-35.

Rows 36-65: Follow colors in Mesh Chart Rows 6-35.

Rows 66-95: Rep Rows 36-65.

Rows 96-118: Follow colors in Mesh Chart Rows 6-28.

Rows 119-123: Follow colors in Mesh Chart Rows 1-5.

Finish off.

VERTICAL STRIPES

Cut 2 strands of black, each 80" long, thread into a large-eyed tapestry needle.

WEAVING

Row 1: Hold afghan horizontally, with starting ch at right-hand side. Starting at ch side, and working toward opposite side, leaving about 5" of yarn loose to be added to fringe, insert needle down through first sp of first row, bring it up through sp of next row, down through sp of next row, continue weaving in this manner to end. Leave the extra yarn at this end to be added to fringe. Pull row of weaving out evenly so mesh does not pucker, then tie weaving strands at each end so they don't pull loose as you work.

For subsequent rows, weave in same manner, alternating up and down position to that of preceding row, following Weaving Row color sequence chart in ***Fig.1***. When first 29-row color sequence is completed, repeat full sequence twice **more**, then work a final 6 rows in black (93 weaving rows in all).

FINISHING

Following Basic Fringe Instructions on page 34, cut 10" strands of yarn in each color. Matching colors to weaving strands, form tassels of 2 strands cut yarn, plus the two strands left from weaving, and knot.
Trim all ends evenly when fringing is completed.

FIG. 1

Background Mesh Row Number	Color Sequence	Weaving Row Number
1—5	Black	1—6
6	Yellow	7
7	Black	8
8	Blue	9
9	Black	10
10—12	Green	11—13
13—14	Red	14—15
15	Black	16
16	Red	17
17	White	18
18	Red	19
19	Black	20
20—21	Red	21—22
22—24	Green	23—25
25	Black	26
26	Blue	27
27	Black	28
28	Yellow	29
29—35	Black	—

BROOMSTICK LACE AFGHAN

Approx. size before fringing: 39" x 58"

MATERIALS

Worsted weight yarn:
Off-White - 36 ounces
Broomstick lace needle, size 50
Crochet hook, size G (Canadian size 7)

Gauge: 5 rows broomstick lace = 6"

Note: If you have worked broomstick lace before, please work a sample swatch from the following instructions. Our method may be slightly different than what you have used before.

BASIC BROOMSTICK LACE

Make a ch as specified in pattern (for practice, ch 10).

Row 1: Holding broomstick needle in left hand, slip loop from crochet hook to needle. Working from **left** to **right** across ch, ★ insert hook into next ch and, being careful not to twist loops, draw up a loop and slip it onto needle ***(Fig. 1)***. Rep from ★ to end of ch: you should have the same number of loops on needle as in the foundation ch.

To work off loops: Insert hook from **left** to **right** through first 5 loops on needle ***(Fig. 2)***; slip these 5 loops off, being careful not to tighten first loop, ch 1 ***(Fig. 3)***; work 4 sc in center of same 5 loops **(one group made, *Fig. 4*)**. ★ Insert hook from **left** to **right** through next 5 loops ***(Fig. 5)***; slip these 5 loops off and work 5 sc in center **(2nd group made, *Fig. 6*)**. Rep from ★ across, do **not** turn.

FIG. 1

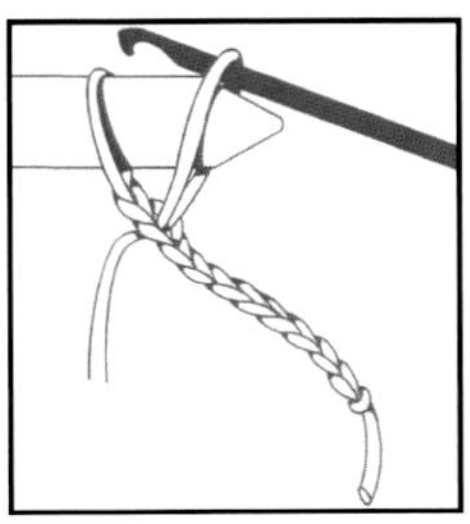

FIG. 2

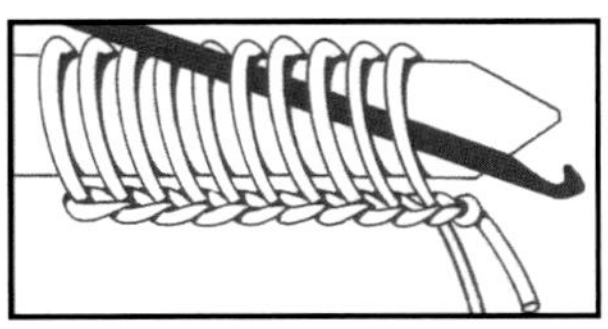

FIG. 3

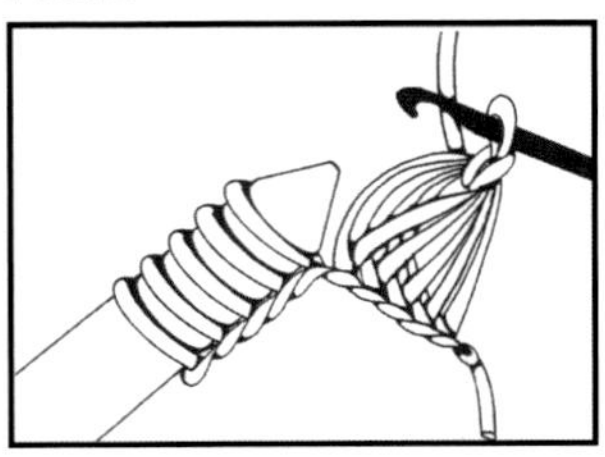

FIG. 4

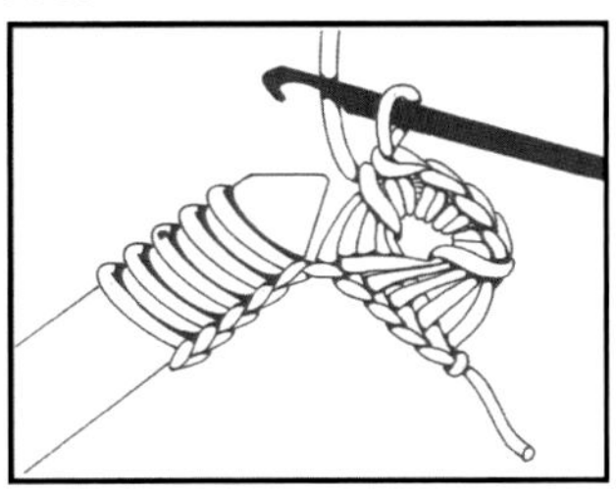

FIG. 5

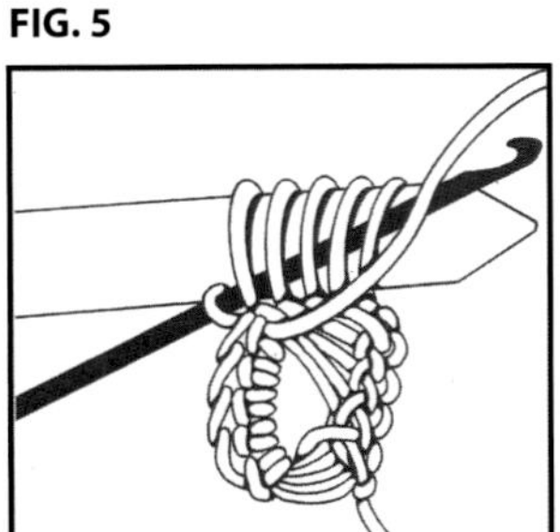

FIG. 6

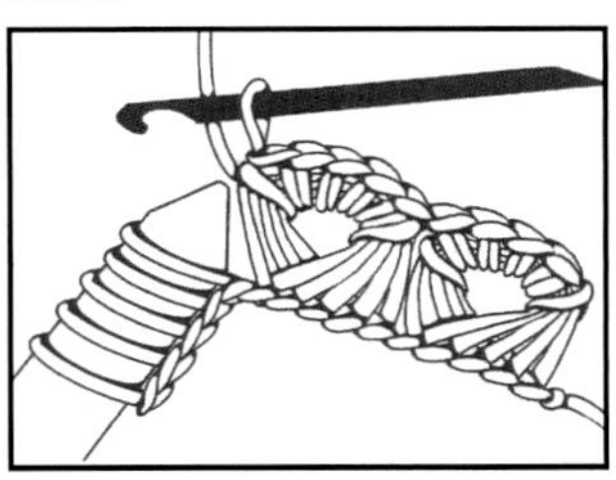

Row 2: Slip loop rem on hook to needle. Working from **left** to **right**, skip first sc,★ hook yarn and draw up a loop in back loop of next sc (loop away from you), ***(Fig. 7)*** and, being careful not to twist loop, slip it onto needle. Rep from ★, ending by drawing up a loop in ch st of last group. There should always be the same number of loops on needle as in the foundation ch. Work off loops in same manner as in Row 1. Rep Row 2 for pattern.

FIG. 7

AFGHAN INSTRUCTIONS

BROOMSTICK LACE PANEL (Make 3)

Ch 40 very loosely.

Following Basic Instructions, work 52 pattern rows (there should be 8 groups in each row), finish off.

EDGING

With **right** side facing, and long edge at top, join yarn with a slip st in upper right-hand corner of one panel.

Row 1: Work 3 sc in each group, and 1 sc in each sc row across ***(Fig. 8)***: 209 sc. Ch 3, turn.

FIG. 8

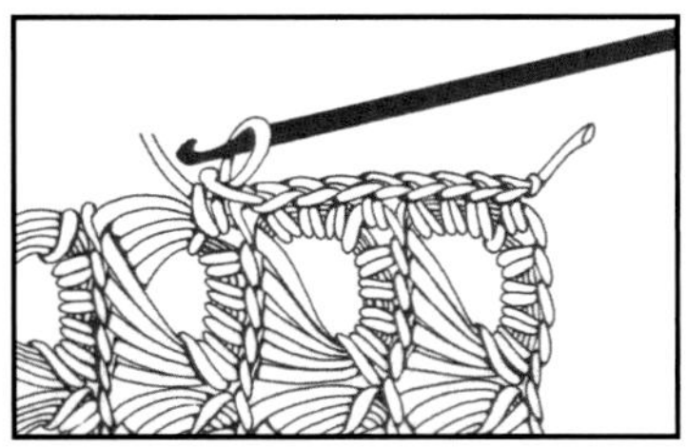

Row 2: Dc in next sc and in each sc across: 209 dc, counting turning ch. Ch 1, turn.

Row 3: Sc in each dc across. Ch 4, turn.

Row 4: ★ skip 1 sc, dc in next sc, ch 1. Rep from ★ across, ending dc in top of turning ch. Ch 1, turn.

Row 5: Sc in each dc and each sp across, ending with sc in 3rd ch of turning ch. Ch 4, turn.

Row 6: Rep Row 4.

Row 7: Sc in each dc and each sp across, ending with sc in 3rd ch of turning ch. Finish off.

With **right** side facing, attach yarn in upper right-hand corner of opposite edge and work Rows 1-7 of edging.

ASSEMBLING

Place 2 strips with **right** sides tog, making sure lace rows go in same direction. Sew strips tog, catching inside thread of each st on each side ***(Fig. 9)***. Join 3rd panel to first 2 in same manner. With **right** side facing, and long edge at top, join yarn in upper right-hand corner. Ch 3, dc in next st and in each st across. Finish off. Rep for opposite side.

FIG. 9

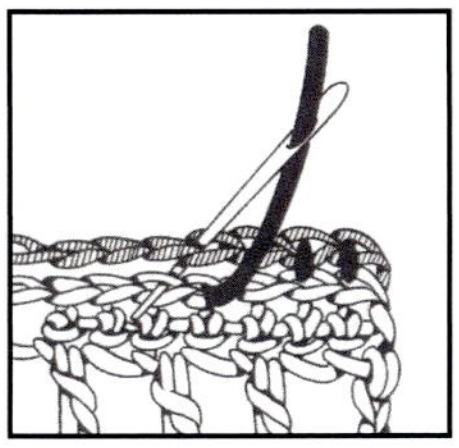

FRINGE

Following Basic Fringe Instructions on page 34, make 48 tassels for each end: one for each group, for each dc row, and for each seam. For each tassel, cut 5 strands 10" long.

SAILBOAT AFGHAN

Approx. size before fringing: 38" x 44"

MATERIALS

Worsted weight yarn:
- White (MC) - 18 ounces
- Navy (Color A) - 10 ounces
- Red (Color B) - 8 oz.

14 " Afghan hook, size J (Canadian size 3) **or** size needed for gauge

Crochet hook, size H (Canadian size 5).

Gauge: In afghan st, 4 sts = 1"; 3 rows = 1"

INSTRUCTIONS

AFGHAN CENTER

With MC and afghan hook, ch 82.

Following Basic Afghan Stitch instructions on page 364, work 77 rows. Work Binding Off row, but do **not** break yarn; change to crochet hook and begin edging.

EDGING

Rnd 1 (Right side)**:** ★ Working into st at end of each row across long edge: 3 sc in first st (corner), sc in each of next 75 sts, 3 sc in last st (corner): 81 sc. Across short edge: Sc in each of first 6 sts, (skip one st, sc in each of next 4 sts) 15 times: 66 sc.
Rep from ★ once **more**, join with a sl st in beg sc; finish off.

Rnd 2: With **right** side facing you, join Color B with a sl st in center sc of any corner 3-sc group. Work (ch 3, 2 dc, ch 1, 3 dc) in same st (corner). † Skip 2 sc, ★ work 3 dc in next sc, sk 2 sc; rep from ★ to center sc of 3-sc group at next corner. Work (3 dc, ch 1, 3 dc) in next sc (corner) †. Rep from † to † 3 times **more**, ending last rep by joining with a sl st in top of beg ch-3; do **not** finish off.

Rnd 3: Sl st to corner ch-1 sp, ch 3, turn. Work (2 dc, ch 1, 3 dc) in same sp. Work 3 dc in sp between each 3-dc group and (3 dc, ch 1, 3 dc) in each corner ch-1 sp around, join with a sl st in top of beg ch-3; finish off.

Rnds 4-24: Continue in same manner, working 2 rnds of **each** color in the following color sequence: MC, Color A, MC, Color B, MC, Color A, MC, Color B, MC, ending by working 3 rnds A. Finish off.

EMBROIDERY

First read Cross Stitch Instructions on page 35. Then thread a tapestry needle with Navy.

Following the boat chart ***(Fig. 1)***, find center (marked) stitch. Now find center stitch on your afghan and begin embroidery at this point. Following the chart, complete the sailboat.

Now work the anchors and diagonal lines in any order you wish.

FRINGE

See Basic Fringe Instructions on page 34. Cut 10" strands of each color. Use 3 strands of White and 1 strand each of Navy and Red for each knot of fringe. Tie one knot in each corner sp and in sp between each 3-dc group across each short end of afghan.

FIG. 1

navy ○

red ♥

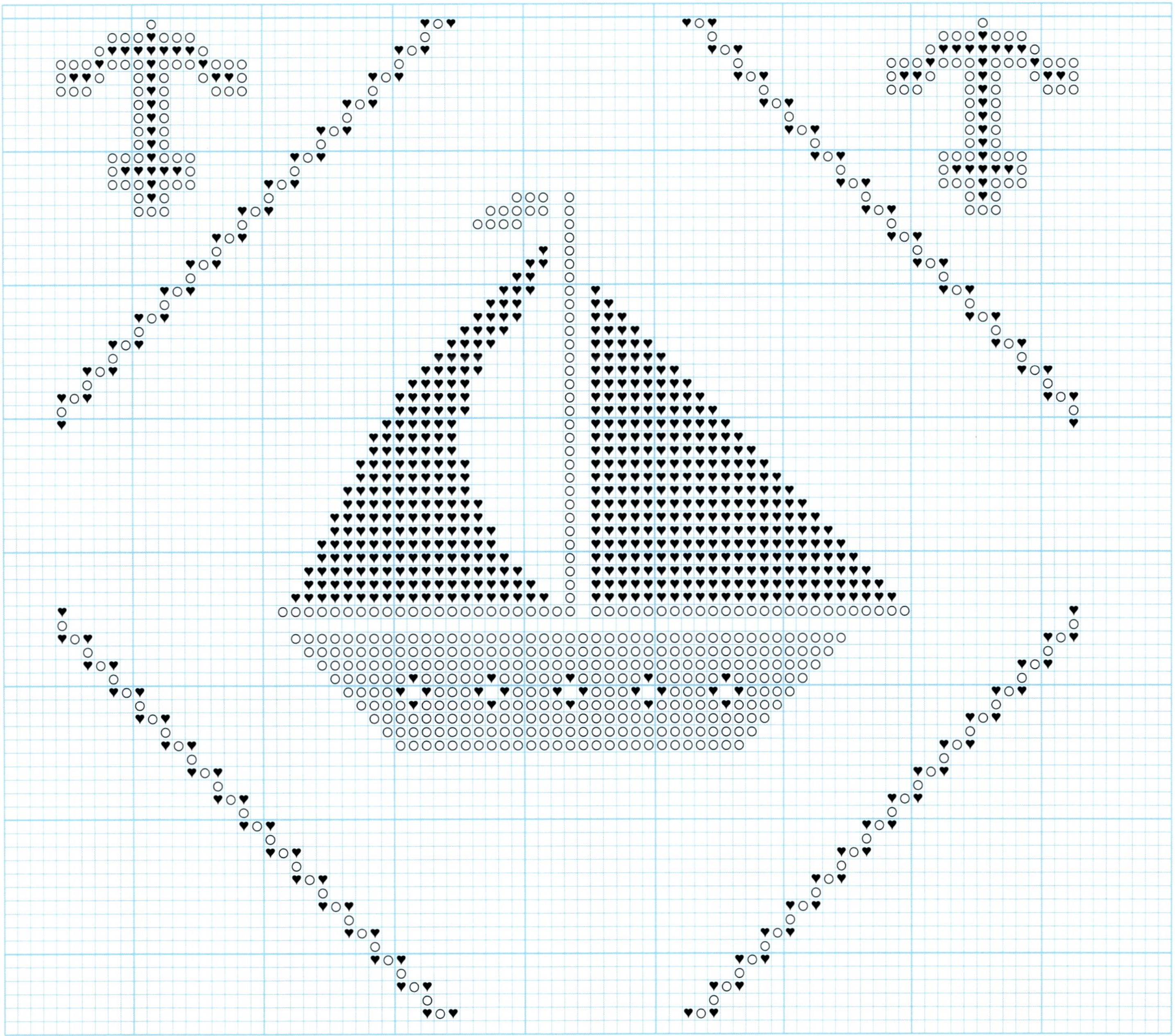

PATCHWORK EMBROIDERED AFGHAN STITCH AFGHAN

Approx. size before fringing: 56" x 72"

MATERIALS

Worsted weight yarn:

Cream - 52 ounces (for background)

For embroidery: Old Gold & Cocoa - 8 ounces **each** color Lt., Med. & Royal Blue; Med. Rose, Burgundy, Orange, Bright Yellow & Lt., Med. & Dk. Olive - 2 oz. **each** color

14" Afghan hook, size J (Canadian size 3) **or** size needed for gauge

Crochet hook, Size H (Canadian size 5)

Gauge: In afghan stitch, 4 sts and 3 rows = 1"

INSTRUCTIONS

Following Basic Afghan Stitch Instructions on page 36, ch 219. Pick up 219 loops and work 217 rows (remember each row consists of two steps). Finish off by working one row of slip st across last row. With H crochet hook, work sc around all four sides, working 3 sc in each corner.

EMBROIDERY

First see Cross Stitch Embroidery section on page 35. Your background piece has 217 sts across, and 217 sts from top to bottom.

To begin, look at chart in ***Fig. 1***, on which center stitch of flower and 22nd Gold st below it are shaded. Now find center stitch on your afghan, and work it in Bright Yellow. You will use this center stitch as the point to start counting as you now lay in, with Old Gold, the outline of the hexagon framework ***(Fig. 2*** shows how this will look when completed).

Thread tapestry needle with one strand of Old Gold. Following ***Fig. 1***, from center stitch, count down to 22nd st below, and make first Gold cross. Continue to work Gold outline around entire center hexagon. In same manner, referring to ***Fig. 1*** to check number of stitches, lay in outline of all other complete and partial (at top and sides) hexagons.

Next, working from ***Fig. 1***, embroider each individual hexagon center. We recommend working from the center hexagon out, but you can start wherever you are most comfortable. In each hexagon, begin in center and work out.

FRINGING

Following the Basic Fringe Instructions on page 34, cut 12" long strands of Cream. Each tassel is composed of 6 strands; tie a tassel in every third stitch across top and bottom. Trim to even off fringe.

FIG. 2

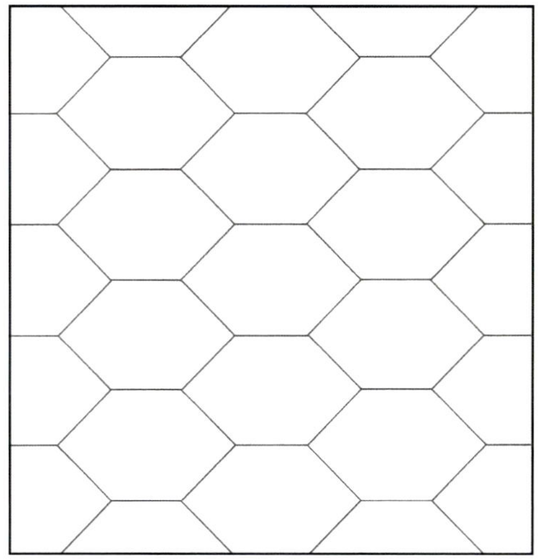

FIG. 1

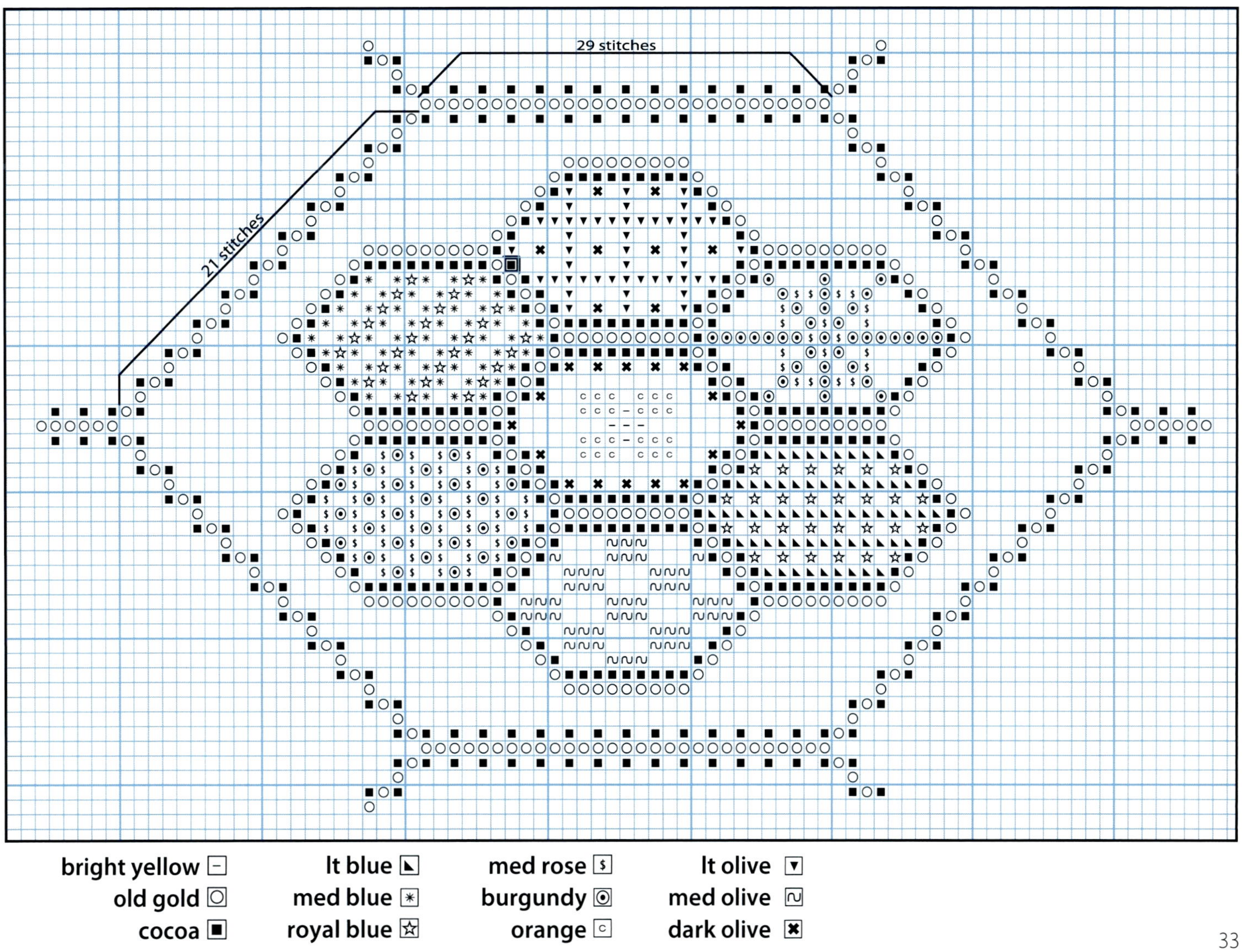

GENERAL INSTRUCTIONS

A NOTE ON BLOCKING

Most of our afghans will not need to be steamed or blocked, however, you may find that your afghan curls at the edges once it is finished. It's also a good idea to steam the seams between afghan panels or granny squares.

You can steam your afghan on the ironing board or on a bed or someplace where it can be spread out. NEVER put the iron down on your work — you can permanently flatten the stitches that way. Instead, hold the iron just above the afghan and the steam will do the work. Once you have steamed one section, let it lie flat for a few minutes, until it is completely dry, then go on to the next section.

JOINING METHODS

On several afghans, you can choose the joining method you prefer for assembling strips or squares. The two following methods are both good; you may wish to practice each and see which you prefer.

Joining Method 1 — Sewing
Place two squares with right sides together. Thread yarn into a tapestry needle. Join yarn securely (no knot, please!) then starting at chain-1 at center of right-hand corner, insert needle in the 2 center loops of each chain and stitch across ***(Fig. 1)***, ending at chain-1 at center of left-hand corner. Fasten yarn off securely.

FIG. 1

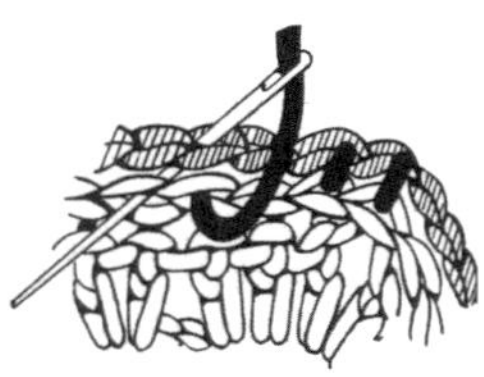

Joining Method 2 — Slip Stitch
Place two squares with right sides together. With yarn, make a loop on hook and join in chain-1 space at center of right-hand corner. Taking care to keep all stitches aligned, slip stitch through ***back loops only*** of each double crochet across side ***(Fig. 2)***, ending with a slip stitch through chain-1 space at center of left-hand corner.

FIG. 2

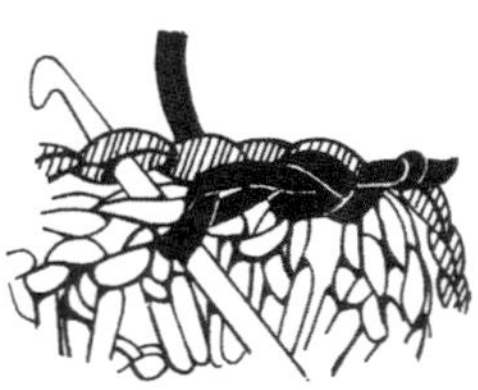

When instructions specify "sew" for joining long strips, you may prefer to use a back stitch, instead of the weaving type of sewing shown above.

BASIC FRINGE INSTRUCTIONS

Cut a piece of cardboard about 6" wide and half as long as specified in instructions for finished strands. Wind yarn loosely around cardboard, cut across one end when card is filled. Cut a big pile of strands and then start fringing; you can wind more strands as you need them.

Fringe with **wrong** side of afghan facing you. Put the number of strands specified for one tassel together and fold in half. With crochet hook draw folded end through space or st ***(Fig. 1)***, pull loose ends through folded section and draw knot up tightly ***(Fig. 2)***. Repeat, spaced as specified in individual afghan instructions. Trim ends to even off.

FIG. 1

FIG. 2

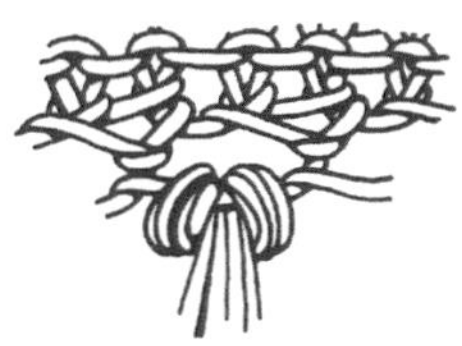

For double fringe knots, after completing fringe as specified above, turn afghan so right side of work is facing you. Work knots as shown in ***Figs. 3 & 4*** across.

FIG. 3

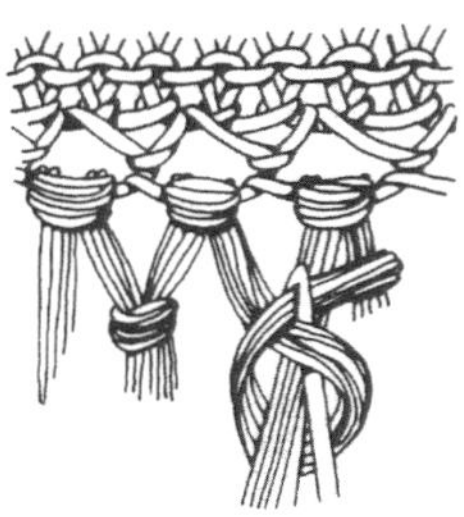

FIG. 4

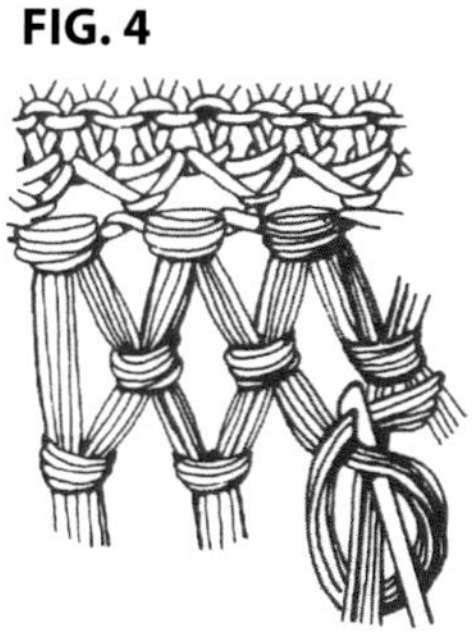

BASIC GRANNY SQUARE

With first color, ch 5, join with a sl st to form a ring.

Rnd 1: Ch 3, 2 dc in ring ***(Fig. 1*** shows first dc being worked in ring), ★ ch 1, 3 dc in ring, rep from ★ twice; ch 1, join to 3rd ch of beg ch-3 with a sl st. Finish off, turn.

FIG. 1

Rnd 2: Attach second color yarn in any ch-1 sp, ch 3, 2 dc ***(Fig. 2*** shows working first dc in space), ch 1, 3 dc in same sp; ★ ch 1, (3 dc, ch 1, 3 dc) in next ch-1 sp, rep from ★ twice, ch 1, join to 3rd ch of beg ch-3 with a sl st. Finish off, turn.

FIG. 2

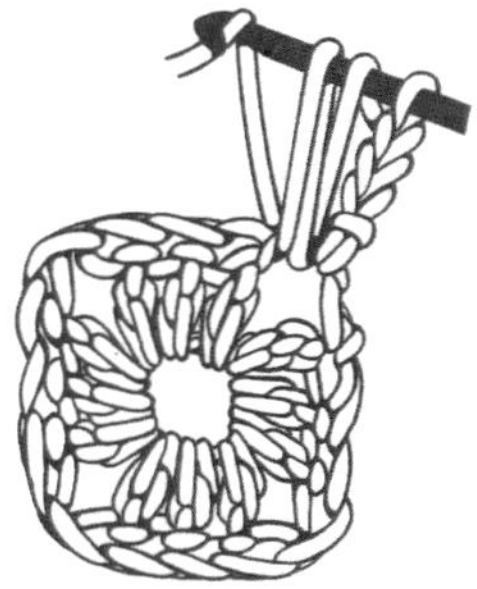

Rnd 3: Attach third color in any corner ch-1 sp, ch 3, 2 dc, ch 1, 3 dc in same sp, ch 1, ★ 3 dc in next ch-1 sp, ch 1; (3 dc, ch 1, 3 dc) in corner ch-1 sp, ch 1, rep from ★ twice; 3 dc, in next ch-1 sp, ch 1, join to 3rd ch of beg ch-3 with a sl st. Finish off, turn.

Rnd 4: Attach yarn in any corner ch-1 sp, (ch 3, 2 dc, ch 1, 3 dc) in same sp, ch 1; ★ (3 dc, ch 1) in each ch-1 sp to corner, (3 dc, ch 1, 3 dc) in corner ch-1 sp, ch 1, rep from ★ twice; (3 dc, ch 1) in each ch-1 sp to corner, join to 3rd ch of beg ch-3 with a sl st.

Rep Rnd 4 with desired colors, until square has number of rnds called for in pattern.

Note #1: When a pattern calls for working 2 or more rnds of the same color in succession, work to end of rnd, do **not** finish off. Sl st to corner sp, ch 3, turn. Continue in pattern, counting ch 3 as starting ch of next rnd.

Note #2: When each square is completed, you'll have lots of yarn ends to be woven in. Make it a practice to weave these in as you finish each square. Otherwise, if you end up with all the squares done, but with all the ends yet to be woven in, you may be horrified!

CROSS STITCH ON AFGHAN STITCH

Several of our most beautiful afghans are first worked in afghan stitch, then embroidered in cross stitch. The embroidery is worked from a chart, on which each square equals one complete cross stitch. On the charts, colors are indicated by symbols.

To work cross stitch on afghan stitch, thread a tapestry needle with an 18" strand of desired color yarn. Do not make a knot. Look at your afghan stitch: note that each upright bar is the center of one stitch: the cross stitches are worked over the bar ***(Fig. 1)***.

FIG. 1

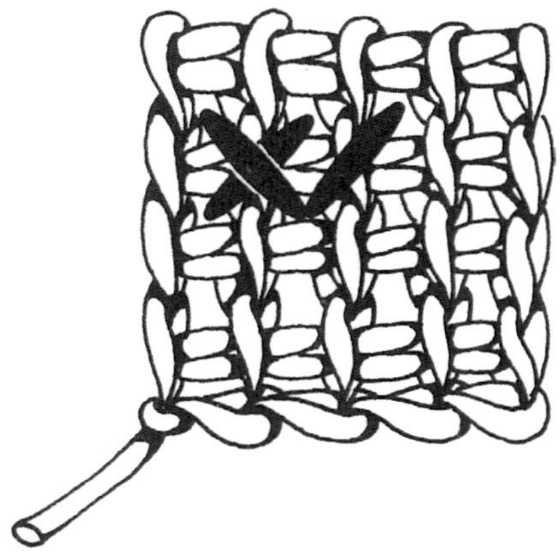

Count to find the stitch with which you wish to begin, bring needle up from back through first hole, leaving a 1" tail of yarn on back to be worked over to secure; bring down in next hole diagonally up, pulling yarn flat against fabric, but not so tight as to pucker fabric.

You have now made one half of a cross stitch; you can either complete that stitch now, or work across area in half crosses, then work back, crossing them as you go. Just be sure the top cross of every stitch goes in the same direction.

To finish off a color, run it through a few stitches on the back.

BASIC AFGHAN STITCH

Just as in regular crochet, all afghan stitch patterns start with a chain. A row of afghan stitch is always done in two steps: first from **right** to **left**, then back again from **left** to **right**.
In instructions, these two steps are considered **one row**.
To practice, ch 14, then follow instructions below, taking care to work loosely. Work until piece measures about 4" long, then bind off as specified below.
In counting rows, Foundation Row ***does*** count as a row.

Foundation Row

First Half: Sk first ch from hook, ★ insert hook through **top loop only *(Fig. 1)*** of next ch, hook yarn and draw through, forming loop on hook (you will now have added a loop). Rep from ★ across ***(Fig. 2)*** to end of ch, keeping all loops on hook.
You should have the same number of loops on hook as the number of chs with which you started. **DO NOT TURN WORK.**

FIG. 1

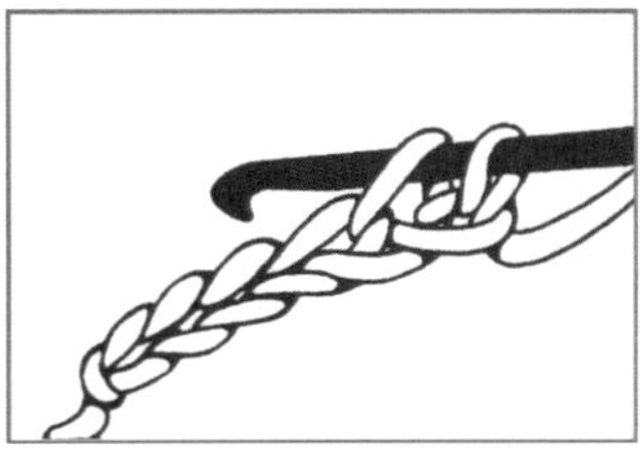

FIG. 2

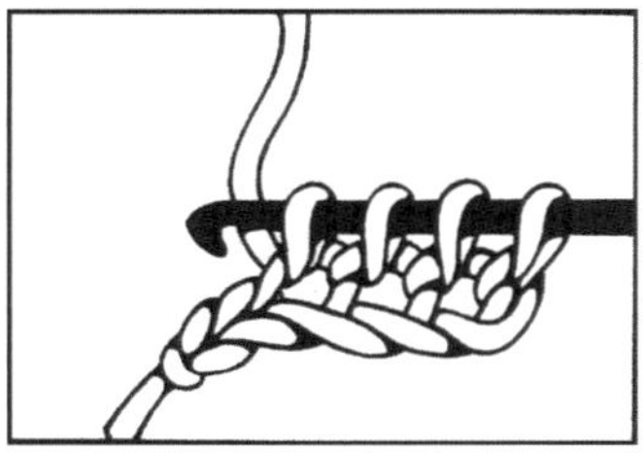

Second Half: YO hook and draw through first loop; ★ YO hook and draw through 2 loops; rep from ★ ***(Fig. 3)*** across row. One loop should remain on hook; this is the first stitch of next row.

FIG. 3

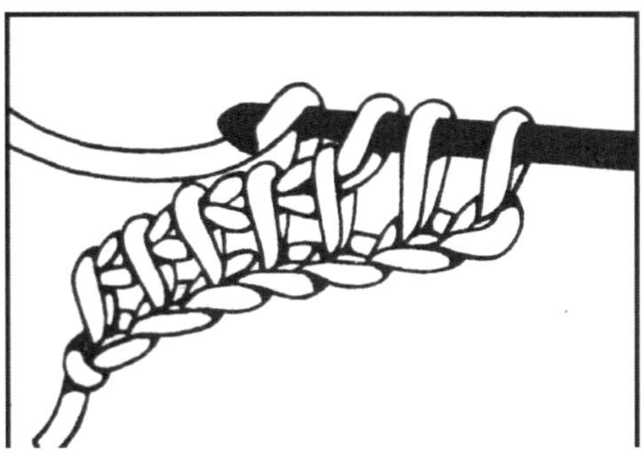

Row 1

First Half: Insert hook in upright part (called a bar) of second st ***(Fig. 4)***; hook yarn and draw through, forming a new loop on hook. Draw up a loop in similar manner in each bar to last bar. On this final bar, for a firmer edge, insert hook in bar **and** thread behind it ***(Fig. 5)***, work them together as one bar. There should still be the same number of loops on hook as the number of starting chs. If you're short a loop, you've probably missed picking up the last bar at the end of the row.

FIG. 4

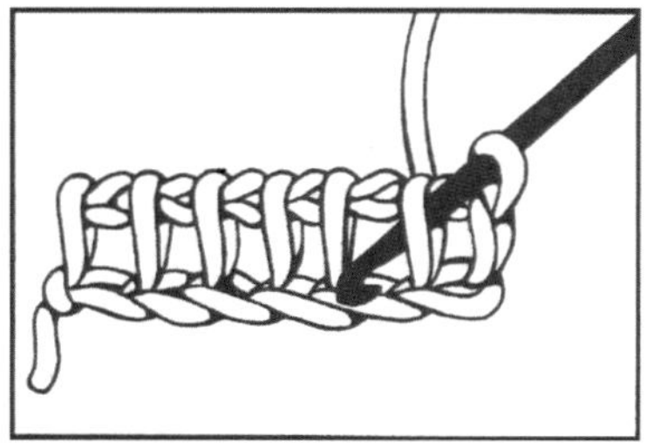

FIG. 5

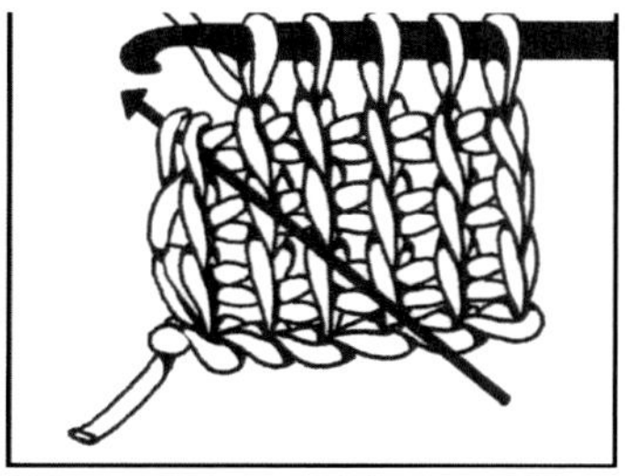

Second Half: Same as Second Half of Foundation Row.
Rep Row 1 for Basic Afghan Stitch.
Your work will begin to look like ***Fig. 6***.

FIG. 6

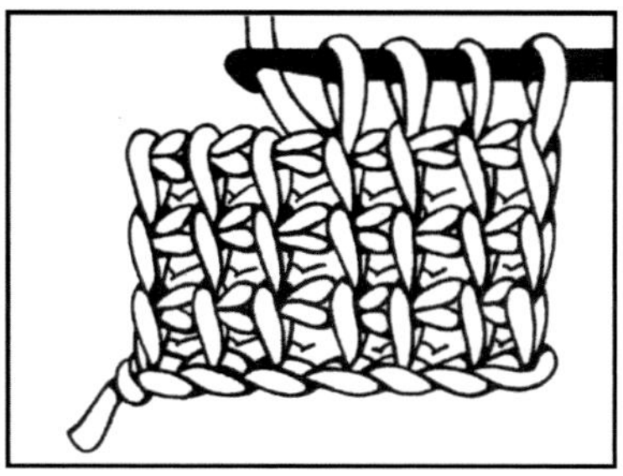

Binding Off: Afghan Stitch is the only crochet stitch that needs to be bound off after the last row.
To bind off, starting on First Half of Row 1, skip first bar, ★ insert hook in next bar, hook yarn and loosely draw through both bar **and** loop on hook: you have made a slip stitch, and just one loop remains on hook; rep from ★ across.
Break yarn, draw through last loop and finish off.

Made in U.S.A.